Contents

Introduction

There is possibly more mystique in finishing than in any of the woodworking skills, and with (arguably) less good reason. Anyone with time and patience can master the encyclopedia of wood finishes and finishing techniques, because manual skill is less important than a painstaking, methodical approach, and an understanding of your materials. French polishers in particular will hate this idea, but there is no intention to belittle their wisdom and experience – just to emphasize that the greatest accomplishment in these crafts is *knowing how your materials behave*, which only comes with practice. Skill with a rubber is not acquired in a day, but learning practical skills like this is within anyone's reach; it doesn't take maths, drawing or accuracy with a saw or chisel, just a feel for the wood and the finish, which no-one can teach you and which you can read in no book.

Beauty and durability are the two characteristics of wood enhanced by an applied coating. If you have seen the potential of an old piece of furniture, realizing its tattiness would be transformed into glory just by a new finish, or if you have laboured long hours over your own construction project and are now looking for the right way to finish it, then the techniques differ only in detail.

Apart from unending patience and a meticulous approach to preparation as well as application, you must also have certain knowledge of what you are mixing with what, in the wood as well as in the can. Different timbers have different chemical characteristics, some reacting violently to materials that will leave others unaffected. You will be using a vast range of chemicals, many of them volatile, and many incompatible one with the other.

Much of wood finishing is common sense. Always read the instructions on containers; always ask suppliers for help if there is something you are not sure of; *never* put a liquid or paste on your precious work if you are unsure what the effect will be. If there is one golden rule of wood finishing, it is *always experiment before applying*.

Finally, the essential ingredient of this, as of all the forms of working wood, is love. Wood responds to your touch and state of mind, becoming implacable if you are impatient, and 'coming up' beautifully if you put care and enjoyment in your fingertips. This is why, however many machine processes you use to get a smooth surface, at the end there is no substitute for using your hands.

Left: *This old-world workshop holds no inaccessible secrets; basic to all wood finishes are patience and a feel for the materials.*

Finishes and stains

Right from the start, be assured there is no perfect wood treatment. All are compromises between durability, appearance, and ease of application, so you must know what final effect you want before you start.

Staining is not always essential. Many craftsmen abhor the use of wood colouring, maintaining that if something is not the right colour, a different wood should have been used in the first place. For refinishing, however, you are bound to be 'matching up'. Dyes and stains have traditionally been used to make cheap wood look better, or to give a uniform appearance to a hodge-podge of timbers in one construction. Different woods behave differently with the same application, so test your colour on inconspicuous parts.

Some stains darken if you put more on; some do not. Some are difficult to apply evenly, but do not fade; some are easy to apply, but are not so light-fast. The actual colouring agent can be a pigment, which does not soak into the wood, or a dye, which does. Finishes also penetrate, or lie on the surface. They dry by evaporation, or by reaction with the air. Waxes and oils are absorbed into the wood, allowing it to breathe and move, and give a warmth unequalled by harder finishes. Oils do not alter the texture of the wood, and waxes, like the scented carnauba and bees' waxes, add their own aroma to a wood's distinctive smell; neither oils nor waxes, however, protect the surface from dents, although some oils are very good for heat and water-

resistance. Waxes need a lot of maintenance; oils give a flat, dull sheen which you do not get with any other finish. Teak and Danish oils contain synthetic resins, which add to their durability and ease of application.

French polish, the shellac finish of tradition, is prized for its clarity, brilliance and depth. It is soft enough to allow the wood to move a little, but it does need protection from liquids and sunlight. While not as difficult to apply as you might think, it requires more processes and a special 'knack'.

There is quite a range of hardness and methods of application even among the varnishes. The traditional types are based on natural resins and gums, the modern ones on synthetic resins – alkyds, phenolics, or polyurethanes. Phenolic-based spar or marine varnish is softer to allow wood movement; polyurethanes are household-hard but difficult to apply well.

Lacquers are either cellulose or synthetic, and because of their speed of drying, most used in furniture production. If you can master spraying – which is not difficult – there is no real reason why they cannot be considered as alternatives to french polish, but it is difficult to apply them with a brush. The vapours they give off are highly noxious, which is perhaps why they do not find their way on to the domestic market. For the purposes of this book, the word 'lacquer' refers to all these finishes.

Left to right: *The high gleam of the french polish on this dressing table may be dulled; light chairs can be given elegance with dark stains; work upwards when staining, keeping one 'live' edge; stripped-pine stain gives new furniture an antique patina.*

Tools and brushes

A lot of edge tools will not be necessary, but for good-quality work they must be sharp. You will need a block plane, preferably with an adjustable mouth, and, perhaps most important in finishing, a cabinet scraper.

Sanding

Sanding blocks made from cork or rubber can be bought, or you can stick a piece of felt or rubber to a block of wood. The block should be big enough to wrap a quarter-sheet of standard-sized abrasive paper around. Apply pumice and rottenstone with a felt-based block.

Sticks and dowels are useful. Wrap the abrasive round ordinary round-section pieces for mouldings, or profile your own for unusual shapes.

Machines can do some of the hard work. Disc sanders for electric drills leave nasty circular scratches. Do not touch them. Belt sanders are heavy, powerful, expensive machines for removing the really rough stuff. A moment's inattention and you will find you have gone right through a veneer or dug a trench in the wood. Rub the (expensive) belts with a wire brush to unclog them. Orbital and finishing sanders are the best bet.

Stripping

Wire (steel) wool is the standard stripping material, and you will also need putty and decorators' filling- and scraping-knives (a hook scraper is efficient but easily scars the surface).

A wire brush will remove every bit of waste from the grain; a small brass shoe-cleaning brush, a nailbrush, and a toothbrush will all be needed at times.

Pointed dowels and toothpicks will all come in useful for carvings and mouldings.

Hot-air strippers make more sense than blowtorches for furniture, but be very gentle. They are best for paint on flat surfaces, and useless for synthetic lacquers. Never use heat to strip veneers.

Brushes

For varnish (which here includes polyurethanes) buy a best-quality 35-50mm (1½-2in.) brush and never use it for anything else. Real bristle is always better than nylon for a good finish. You need full bristles, slightly tapered, with some flagged tips to control the flow. In cheap brushes, the two rows of bristles are set too wide apart to hold the liquid and let it flow well.

Fine artist's brushes will be necessary for touching in colours; bear-, sable- or squirrel-hair 'mops' for shellac in awkward corners and a 'grass' or nylon scrubbing brush for bleaches. The finest is a 'dulling' brush (furniture rubbing brush), for laying pumice powder on to a bright finish. See pp. 56-7 for advice on brush care.

Brushes should always be finest quality. You will need artist's brushes, and a first-class varnish brush; the wire brush is indispensable for stripping.

Orbital sanders move in 3mm (⅛in.) circles, which can leave scratches that you do not see until the finish is on; finishing tools move straight back and forth.

Repairs

Minor repairs demand a tenon or dovetail saw, sharp chisels, block plane, and a selection of the invaluable G-cramps (clamps).

For veneer work, add a scalpel or other sharp, thin-bladed knife, a veneer saw and an electric iron.

The cabinet scraper

A favourite finisher's tool, the cabinet scraper is merely a rectangular piece of tool steel which can take four sharp edges. It will produce a smooth cut, however wild the grain is, which is why it is indispensable for work on veneers with decorative, curly grain.

To use the scraper, hold it in both hands, with your thumbs in the middle, flexing it and pushing away from you at a 45° angle to the surface. It should produce a shaving and leave a very smooth surface. If you get dust, it is blunt; if the grain cuts up rough, push it the other way. It can heat up very quickly and burn your thumbs, so take a slight warmth as a warning.

To sharpen the scraper, the thin edge must be dead square to the flat face, and dead straight. Hold it in a vice (vise) and draw a flat file along the edge to get the right angle. You have to produce a burr and wipe (curl) it back – it is the burr itself that cuts. Draw the edge back and forth on an oilstone, keeping it absolutely square to the stone, or trap it between the two halves of the box and rub on the stone's edge, if you have one in a box. When you feel a burr on both sides of the edge, lay it flat on the bench and strop it with a round piece of spring steel or the back of a gouge (the ticketter/ burnisher). This brings the burr over in line with the flat face, so the ticketter must be flat to that face.

Now hold the scraper on end on the bench and pad your hand with a cloth. Run the ticketter up the narrow edge, angling it back towards the flat face very slightly. Do this three or four times on all the corners, angling the ticketter back slightly more each time till it is at about 70°-80° to the flat. Try the cut; if you get dust not shavings, take it back to the stone.

Old finishes are hard, and will blunt this burr quite quickly. The last two ticketter stages will 'dress' the cutting edge again, but after three or four times, you will need to take it back to the stone.

The cabinet scraper

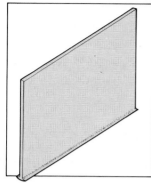

1 The scraper cuts with a burr on the narrow edges.

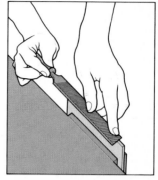

2 To sharpen, draw a flat file along the edge.

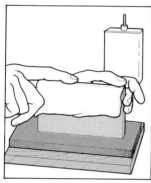

3 Draw the edge back and forth on an oilstone.

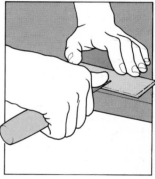

4 Lay it flat and strop it with the ticketter.

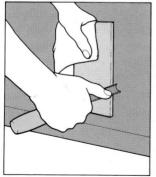

5 Run the ticketter up the narrow edge.

6 A sharpened scraper produces shavings, not dust.

Abrasives and adhesives

A clear finish may sometimes disguise or obscure the grain, but it will *never* cover imperfections in the surface of the wood. Rather, it will emphasize them. The more work you put into sanding, the better your chances of a first-class finish.

Abrasives

Abrasive papers are made from glass (flint), flour, garnet, aluminium oxide or silicon carbide. Glasspaper is the cheapest, but it also wears out quickest. It has no real advantages over garnet, which gives a more 'sympathetic' cut, and hardwoods seem to like it better. Aluminium oxide papers are expensive, long-lasting, and are usually used with machines. Silicon carbides (wet and dry), though available in coarse grades, tend to be used for cutting back between coats, especially of hard synthetic lacquers. Lubricate them with water, white spirit (paint thinner) or mineral oil. Avoid using liquid paraffin or mineral oil, which are insoluble in meths (wood alcohol), on raw wood. Raw linseed oil is usually better.

There are at least three marking systems, of which the easiest one is the 'ordinary' numbers, starting at 30 or 40 for the coarsest grades. A 30/40 grit size is the same as S2 for the glass and 1½ for the garnet; 100 grit is F2, 2/0 garnet; and 150 is 1 glass, 4/0 garnet.

Black silicon carbide is best for smoothing an already finished surface; red garnet papers suit hardwoods very well.

Steel wool is used for stripping in nooks and crannies where no tool blade will go, for surface repairs and reviving, for cutting back between coats, and for final burnishing, usually with wax or oil. The coarsest grade available is 3, the very finest is 0000 or 4/0.

Pumice and rottenstone are fine powders – pumice is the coarser – usually mixed with oil to make an abrasive burnishing paste. The friction they create is also an effective remover of blemishes in shellac finishes.

Car polishes, including T-Cut, can be used. Any really fine abrasive paste, even toothpaste, is good in the last burnishing stages.

Adhesives

Animal (scotch) glue was about the only furniture adhesive there was until the 1950s, and you are bound to come across it in repairs. It is used hot, and can be melted – with care – with hot water or an iron to make it stick again.

PVA (yellow) is the most commonly used adhesive nowadays. While not waterproof, it is extremely strong. Time and pressure are needed for it to set effectively.

Formaldehydes are usually bought in powder form and mixed with water for application. They are harder to use than PVA, but are waterproof.

Impacts (contacts) are good for sheet materials but unforgiving because they stick immediately, unless you use a 'thixotropic', which allows some re-positioning.

Two-pack epoxies set rock-hard. They are useful for filling and building up in woodwork.

Safety, comfort and conditions

Most of the materials you will be using are highly flammable, highly corrosive, or both. Do not smoke; do not leave saturated rags lying about; always put the caps back on containers, and store them where they will not be knocked over. Label the jars in which you keep your own concoctions, noting the exact proportions of the mix so you can reproduce them. You will *want* a face mask when you use acid-catalysed lacquers, never mind need one, but it is easier to be lazy about eye protection when you are stripping. Splashes go a lot further than you think and it is not worth risking damage. Rubber gloves are a must for these liquids too, although if you wear them for french polishing you will lose the feel of the rubber. Shellac, although not harmful to the skin, is no cosmetic, and you just might discover some interesting allergies.

Dust is your major enemy. Any sticky surface is like fly-paper, and once dust sticks, you will only do more damage to the finish trying to get it off. You can only really guarantee a dust-free atmosphere if you work in an operating theatre, or have got an extraction system, but there are ways of minimizing it; aim not to disturb it, rather than to be completely rid of it. You need good ventilation for your lungs' sake and for drying, but try to arrange it so the air does not cause draughts near the work, or bring dust in from outside the room. Damp the floor and sweep it thoroughly, then lay your cloths or newspapers – polythene (plastic) sheeting is melted by strippers and many of the finishes – and do not sweep again until the finish is completely dry.

For your own comfort and the sake of the finish, the workspace must be neither hot nor cold, and certainly not damp. Moisture creates 'bloom' (a white haze) in french polish, which also will not harden below about 18°C (65°F). Varnishes and lacquers, on the other hand, dry too quickly if they are too hot; a skin forms which prevents the reaction with the air, and they do not harden underneath.

Light is also important. Work near a window if possible so you can see exactly what you are doing, and do not fool yourself about imperfections in the surface.

Be methodical, be patient, and do not hurry. Allow time to get started and to clear up. Always add one-third to your estimate of how long something will take, and you will not be far off. Impatience is a guarantee of eventual dissatisfaction, and more than likely a lot of time wasted redoing a finish. Your standards are up to you, but you are unlikely to be reading this if you do not think something worth doing is worth doing well.

You can never, of course, have enough space in a workshop. This small area is neatly arranged and well-lit: note the trestles, padded for protection, and the clearly labelled jars.

Preparation

Recognizing the finish and deciding to strip

The first refinishing decision you will have to make is whether you need to strip the entire piece. A scruffy, dirty finish does not automatically need stripping; basically, as long as there are not too many scratches and they are not too deep, there are quite a few ways to avoid going back to the bare wood.

Clean your piece thoroughly with detergent and warm water, and, perhaps, use a mild abrasive like steel wool. Try not to get the surface too wet, particularly veneer, which will lift if water gets under it. Shellac and lacquer cloud if water is left lying on them. White spirit (paint thinner) or methylated spirits (wood alcohol) will shift stubborn grime, but be careful – if the rag is really soaked, it could start dissolving the finish.

To establish what the finish is, test an inconspicuous part with solvents. Meths will dissolve french polish, which will set again, but varnish will merely crinkle and lift. Cellulose and the acid lacquers will soften and set again when treated with their own solvents (thinners), but meths alone will not affect them. Scraping with a chisel is another way of distinguishing varnish from cellulose; varnish comes off in a yellow shaving, the lacquers make white dust. A certain amount of common sense helps you narrow the options, in that a battered antique is obviously not going to have a thoroughly modern finish. Once you know what you have, use a cleaner that will not dissolve it.

If the finish is basically intact, sand it with fine paper or steel wool and prepare it for a new coat of the same thing. If, however, it is worn right through, chipped, and peeling, you will need to remove it all. Sometimes the top of a table or sideboard is badly damaged, and the rest is sound, in which case it is possible to strip and recoat just the top, although matching colours could be a problem. Crazing and cracks in french polish and lacquered surfaces can be healed, if they are not too deep, by reamalgamation (see pp. 26-7). If you are going to be repairing the wood in any way, clean the finish off around where the repair will be, but wait till the gluing and clamping are over before stripping completely.

Left: *From flat and dull to a rich colour and a deep sheen . . . be meticulous in removing every trace of old finish. This table has been stained and varnished; the curved front is veneered.*

Stripping

There are basically three stripping methods open to you – sanding, heat and chemicals – and you will probably find yourself using at least two, whatever the piece. Regardless of the method(s) you intend to use, you will find it easier to take the piece apart as far as possible: remove drawers, fittings, shelves and so on and treat them all separately.

Because it is mechanical, sanding is a more controlled way of stripping, but it is unlikely that you will be able to remove everything, especially from the nooks and crannies, without chemical help. The belt sander's power and weight is ideal when you have a lot of layers to get through, especially paint, but it really is not the right tool for valued pieces of furniture.

You can use heat, although a blowlamp (blowtorch) is far too violent for furniture. The hot-air strippers popular nowadays are more gentle, but it is still all too easy to burn the wood if you look away for so much as a second. Bubble up the paint and lift it off with a decorator's knife, layer by layer. Heat does not really work on french polishes and lacquers, except for the highly risky business of flashing, a trade practice that involves wiping a meths-soaked rag over french polish and setting it alight. It *is* very effective, but the risks are obvious!

Chemicals are most efficient, and do the least damage to the wood, but bear in mind that they and their waste are highly flammable; that they are very harmful to skin and eyes, so you must wear goggles and rubber gloves; and that you *must* neutralize them.

Proprietary strippers are usually methylene chloride based; pastes are generally a better idea than liquids, because they stick to vertical surfaces. Dab the stripper on with a grass or nylon brush, or a dispensable paint brush and dollop it, rather than brushing. The idea is to leave a thickness that will soak in and lift up the old finish; putting it on too thick or leaving a thick coat over-long does not increase the product's efficiency. Work layer by layer, scraping with a knife, or wire wool for awkward bits.

Ready-made strippers are usually neutralized by water or white spirit, which dissolves the wax that some of them use to prevent quick drying. Remember that if you get old furniture and veneers too wet, you will melt the glue. Some strippers are promoted as 'no-wash', which is useful, but (apart from veneers) there can be no harm in wiping over with water or white spirit.

Caustic soda is still popular, if not so easy to use as proprietary strippers. It needs to be thickened into a paste with whiting, starch or even wallpaper paste, and used as strong as you dare to avoid the water wetting the wood too deeply. A kilo (2-3lb) of crystals to a bucket of water should give the right consistency. Do not use it on veneered pieces, and remember to mix the crystals into the water, not the other way round. It also darkens the fibres, which will need to be bleached out again (see pp. 38-9). Neutralize it with vinegar.

There are commercial stripping firms, who use large tanks of caustic solution in which the whole piece is submerged; this 'dipping' is an easy alternative to taking the work on yourself. It is good for, say, a staircaseful of balusters, but the trisodium phosphate darkens the wood, damages the fibres, and attacks the glue in joints. It is also unlikely that your furniture will be given the careful treatment you would give it yourself, and naturally everything you give an operator is given at your own risk.

You will often find a white deposit in the grain of mahogany furniture that will not come out when you have stripped the piece. This is plaster of paris, used as a grain filler, that has hardened; scrub it out with a wire brush and linseed oil, and resign yourself to a lot of sanding and smoothing afterwards.

Stripping

1 Dab on stripper with an old paint brush.

2 Lift paint off layer by layer with a decorator's knife.

Repairs to existing veneers

Although a discussion of the numerous repairs you are likely to come across in revitalizing old furniture is beyond the scope of this book, it is useful to know how to treat and patch veneers and surfaces.

There is much more veneer around than you might think. Before the days of manufactured boards, pine was often overlaid with mahogany as an inexpensive way of making expensive-looking furniture. If it is chipped or blistered, it will be easy to identify as veneer, but if it is still in good condition, you can tell by looking for the telltale thin edge at the back of, say, a chest of drawers, or checking inside a cabinet or underneath a table to see whether the grain and colour of the wood are different.

Older items will be glued with animal (scotch) glue, which can be softened and made to stick again with heat. If the veneer has lifted at an edge, try to see if the glue is crumbly and crystalline by poking it gently with a thin blade. If it is granular, scrape it out as far back as you can without splitting the loose piece and scrape the 'ground' – the base wood – to uncover a raw surface, then slide a blade or piece of card with some white (yellow) glue on it to coat both surfaces, and clamp it with a G-clamp. If the glue has not broken up completely, heat it gently with an iron through several thicknesses of brown paper (*not* newspaper). Keep testing as it softens and once it has become sticky, clamp the loose piece down.

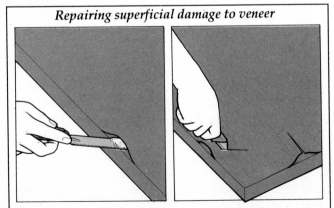

Repairing superficial damage to veneer

1 At an edge, slide in glue with a palette knife.

2 Make one cut along or diagonally across the grain.

Treating bubbles in veneer

1 Cut an X-shape diagonally across the grain.

2 Lift the veneer and carefully scrape out the old glue.

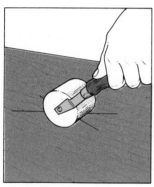

3 Roll the surface flat with a wallpaper edge-roller.

4 Put a heavy weight over it until the new glue is dry.

Blistering or bubbling in the middle of a surface is another common phenomenon. If the veneer is not chipped, cut it with a razor-sharp blade like a scalpel, from edge to edge of the lifted part. Try the iron and brown paper first; roll the veneer flat and weight it down to set with a heavy weight on some greaseproof paper. (This will stop the weight sticking to the veneer and pulling it up again when you take it off.) If the old glue does not work, you will have to scrape it out and reglue. Be as delicate as you can – veneer is brittle at the best of times, and it is going to be messier if you break a piece and have to glue that as well. Slide the new glue in with an artist's palette knife or something similar. When the glue has set, sand it smooth and refinish.

Veneer, marquetry and solid wood patching and replacement

Often in a veneered surface there are pieces missing, which need to be replaced. Inlay lines and marquetry pieces tend to shrink and become loose so although specialist suppliers keep a wide range of ready-made inlays, be careful ordering the size. It is safer to order oversize, and reduce the insert by rubbing the edge on 120 grit sandpaper laid on the bench. Replacements for marquetry panels may need specialist identification; keep the piece you remove to use as a pattern.

When you have a good piece of matching veneer, plan a patch so that the grain and figure blend in as

Patching veneer

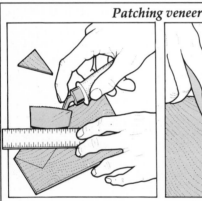

1 Cut a diamond-shaped patch with a veneer saw.

2 Mark around the patch, bevelling the edges inwards.

3 Cut away the veneer inside the marks.

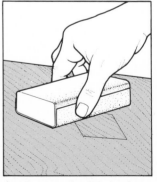

4 When the glue has dried, sand the patch flush.

closely as possible. Cut a piece slightly larger than the damaged area. A veneer saw is the most reliable tool for cutting brittle veneers; even the sharpest of knife-blades can drag along an edge and pull a chip of grain out. The diamond should be lengthwise on the grain, to avoid obvious repair lines going across. Clean out the waste with a chisel, bevel downwards, back to the lines. Fit the patch tightly, using a file or garnet paper to reduce it, working *with* the grain. The points of the diamond are extremely fragile. When the piece is a perfect fit, coat both the surface and the veneer with white glue, position the patch and weight it to set.

Solid patches are cut in much the same way. You will need to chisel out a depression to hold the patch, but the fit along the edges is much more important than the flatness of the gluing surface. Anything less than razor-sharp tools will pull the edges of the repair down rather than cut them, and make the patch very noticeable. As with veneers, the repair should be slightly proud of the surface when you set it in, so you can sand it back flush when the glue has dried. Letting pieces into an edge also demands that you fit an oversize piece and plane and shape it back to blend after the glue has set.

A dent in raw wood can often be steamed out. A hot iron on a damp cloth can swell the fibres enough to bring the surface level. Try once and repeat if it does not work; if the dent is too deep, you might have to wax fill it (see pp. 24-5). If you have to prick the surface, fill the holes later with wax or shellac stick.

Treating surface damage to raw wood

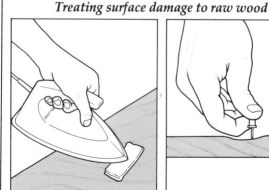

1 *A hot iron on a damp cloth can steam out a dent.*

2 *If the dent is under a finish, prick the finish, then steam it.*

Treating superficial damage to a finish

If the wood itself is not damaged beyond the scope of a filler or stopper, but the finish has generally deteriorated, there are numerous remedies.

For localized problems like shallow scratches, try furniture polish, shoe polish, or even the kernel of a nut to wet, darken and blend the lighter area. Often it is only a matter of colour, and ordinary wax crayons work very well in small amounts. You can get different colours by mixing and melting shavings. The more specialized wax and shellac sticks are good for deep blemishes, even those that have gone right through to the wood. They have to be heated on a hot knife-blade – preferably curved – and dripped into the scar, then smoothed over while they are still warm, but left proud of the surface and sanded back when hard. Paint in grain lines before the finish coat. Do not hold these sticks in the flame – they are highly flammable.

White rings or spots, an overall 'bloom', or a smoky blue haze are common results of damp in or on french polish and cellulose. If a general bloom does not disappear when wiped (hard) with white spirit, camphor oil and tobacco ash, or meths, then it is likely that the damp is under the finish, which will have to be stripped. Be careful with meths – if your rag is too damp you will dissolve shellac. The smoky blue effect is usually the result of wax or oil being rejected by a silicone polish beneath; upper and lower layers are usually easily dealt with by white spirit.

Shellac stick

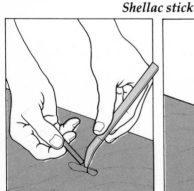 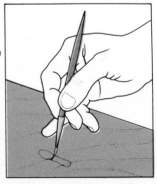

1 Melt the stick and drip it into the scar.

2 Paint in grain lines with a fine brush and oil paints.

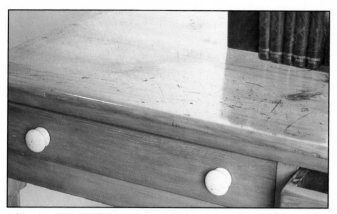

This pine table has been re-varnished, but the scratches and marks of age have been left under the finish.

The way to deal with the white rings or blushes that have been caused by cups and glasses, or other damp from on top, is friction. Start with the finest abrasive, even 'extra bright' toothpaste, and get progressively stronger if you get no result. Abrasive car polish, rottenstone or pumice powder mixed with mineral oil and rubbed on with a felt pad, salt with oil, salt with vinegar and fine steel wool and oil all abrade, and some have a chemical action as well. If you rub patiently, after a while the finish will be re-fused by the friction.

Buff the area, which will now be much duller, with a soft cloth, and apply wax or oil, unless you intend to renew the whole finish.

In apparently severe cases, check that the wood itself is also damaged.

Repairing more severe damage to a finish

Chips and holes in a varnished or french polished surface can be built up by applying a 'touch-in' of the same finish in the depression, letting it dry, and adding more until you bring it level. For huge gashes, make cellulose 'jam' by pouring a capful of cellulose lacquer into a tin lid, letting it evaporate to become sticky, adding a bit more and letting that dry out, and so on. This is an ideal thick filler for damage to cellulose surfaces. Use a fine artist's brush, and make sure your previous coat is hard before you apply the next one.

A scuffed, dull surface with multiple light scratches can be brought back into condition with fine steel wool (000 or 0000) and mineral oil, rubbed in the direction of the grain. Wipe the oil off, then wax or furniture polish the surface. You can buy french polish 'revivers', which should be applied in the same way and buffed, first with steel wool and wax and then a soft cloth.

For even more severe deterioration of french polish and cellulose, reamalgamate the finishes with their respective solvents. Varnish will not respond to this treatment because it hardens by reaction rather than evaporation, as do the acid lacquers. For french polish, soak fine steel wool in meths and rub it along the grain so that both the liquid and the action fuse the surface. This needs a delicate touch; you have to dissolve the finish enough to move it around, but not so much as to create ridges or inadvertently strip it. Wipe the meths off with a rag before the finish starts to go. The same method works for cellulose using thinners. If cellulose is badly cracked, paint the thinners along the lines with a fine brush and fuse it by pushing gently with the heel of your hand before you wipe the solvent over.

Left: *Remove burns and charring by scraping the area from side to side with a sharp blade held upright.*

Right: *Scratches and burns on this table have broken the finish and affected the wood. Use wire wool and stripper (far right) to remove as many marks as you can, then scrape, fill and touch in.*

Reamalgamation

1 For cellulose, paint thinners along the cracks.

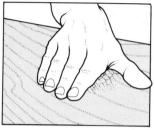

2 Fuse it by pushing with the heel of your hand.

3 For french polish, use steel wool and meths.

4 Wipe the meths off with a rag.

A professional's trick for reamalgamating is flashing, in the same way as described for stripping french polish on pp. 18-19, but with the important addition of a wiped layer of mineral oil before you apply the meths. The finish softens and moves, but is not burned off because of the protective oil. Have the surface vertical so the flame travels upward, work quickly, and take every fire precaution.

Sanding

There is quite a difference between sanding bare wood and 'rubbing down', 'cutting' or 'flatting back' between coats. Apart from where you are removing blemishes, always work from coarse to fine; for raw wood range from 100 to 120/150 to 240/320 grit. Final sanding on a top coat can require 600 grit wet and dry, if you have the patience. Do not skimp on sanding – no-one ever got a perfect finish without meticulous attention to it.

Machines take a lot of the hard work out of a potentially boring job, but sympathetic hand-sanding is always necessary at the last stage. A belt sander worked diagonally across the grain then along it cuts a rough surface like new pine very quickly; a hand block also works well like this, but you will give yourself extra work if the surface is already quite smooth. Orbital and finishing sanders are safer, if slower, than the belt machines although the tiny circular scratches can be a bugbear. Get a machine with dust extraction, or stop every minute or two to brush the dust off.

The question of 'cleaning off' before you stain and finish is a vital one. Wipe the work over with white spirit or, best of all, use a 'tack rag' – a soft cloth soaked in water, the finish you are using, and its solvent, then squeezed out. The dust adheres to the stickiness of the rag, rather than being pushed around on the surface.

'Between-coat' sanding is a matter of flattening ridges and imperfections, removing dust stuck in the coat, and providing a 'key' for the next layer. Use the finest grades of garnet or wet and dry paper, lubricated

When hand-sanding open-grained softwood, use a coarse grit diagonally, then straight, then follow the grain's pattern.

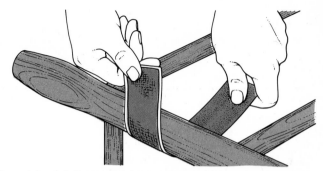

Use a strip of cloth tape stuck to sandpaper for round components.

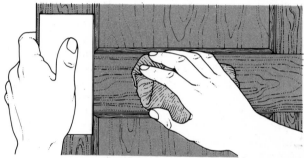

Where grain meets at right angles, avoid scratches by covering the area you're working towards with card.

with water or oil. The sludge created is itself an excellent abrasive. Use your fingertips to judge the results, and look along the surface in angled light.

Steel wool is used for stripping awkward areas, a fine cut between coats, and – lubricated with wax or oil – burnishing the final coat. The finer the scratches, the smoother the finish, until it gets to the point where you are creating a gloss, not dulling it.

Car polishes are good for final perfection and durability, but they do contain silicon; pumice or rotten-stone powder, applied with oil by felt pad, will get the last specks out of your satin finish, and applied dry and very lightly with a 'dulling brush' (furniture rubbing brush) will bring a high-gloss finish down in brilliance.

In these super-fine stages, be careful about the direction of your movements. It is tempting to assume that the abrasive is so fine that you can rub round in a buffing action, but even those minute scratches will reflect light in different directions and you will see them as marks, so stay in parallel lines with the grain.

Stains

If you are doing any refinishing you will certainly be using wood stains, and if you are making new items from scratch, sooner or later you will want to alter the colour of the wood in some way. You need to know the best stains for your particular needs; terms can be confusing, in that an 'oil' stain has a (usually naphtha) base, soluble in white spirit (paint thinner), while a 'spirit' stain uses not white but methylated spirit (wood alcohol) as its solvent medium.

You might want to enliven wood, deepening and enriching the colour; to emphasize the 'figure', or pattern of the grain; to give, say, new mahogany the characteristic rich red brown of antique furniture – to make any new wood look old, in fact. You might need to match new repair wood to the colour of old existing parts, or want to disguise a wood entirely, giving inexpensive pine the appearance of much dearer timbers like oak. Stains do all of these, and always have.

Whatever stain you are using, for whatever purpose, *never do it without testing first.*

It is important to know when you are using stain that different woods absorb at different rates, and that parts of the same piece of wood will behave differently. Be aware, when you are dealing with furniture with curved components, or staining a banister, for instance, that absorbency differs as the grain meets the surface at a constantly varying angle. There is nothing so annoying as uneven patches in a piece over which you have taken a lot of care; some of the ways to avoid this patchiness are dealt with on pp. 34-5.

Careful preparation is vital. Allow more time than you think you need, and if you are mixing to match, make more than you think you need, rather than be caught with too little to finish the job. Pay particular attention when sanding to patches of grease or old finish, which collect in the awkward corners where you cannot get them off, but which show up disproportionately when you apply the colour. Be patient!

Water, oil and spirit are all used to carry the two basic colouring agents – pigments, which do not penetrate deeply, and dyes, which do. There is no stain to lighten wood – for that you must use bleach (see pp. 38-9).

Left: *For recolouring to period style after stripping and restoring, or just matching neighbouring furniture, you will probably have to mix stain shades. Make sure the solvent bases of the materials are compatible.*

Pigmented stains

Pigments in oil – in this case, white spirit (paint thinner) or naphtha – were originally used for graining effects, and indeed still are, which is why they are called 'wiping stains'. They can be used for raw wood. The more common pigmented stains use a water-soluble medium, and are available on the DIY market as 'wood colour' (wood stains). Coloured varnishes carry pigments too, insoluble particles in an oil/resin medium.

These stains are not easy to apply evenly, because the particles of colour stay on the surface or are absorbed with marked variation in rate and depth. Endgrain and open grain end up darker, as do scratches and blemishes; while hard knots remain unaffected, the wild grain around them is especially absorbent. The ranges are easy to mix and inexpensive, but not suitable for the close-grained hardwoods.

Water-based products raise the grain of the wood so you will have to sand after staining, which will certainly remove some of the pigment. This is fine if you want areas of shading, such as in the corners of a panel, but otherwise it is annoying, so once the stain is dry, but *before sanding*, seal it with an extremely thin coat of the clear finish you intend to use. Otherwise, rub down, wet the surface, then sand it again before you stain it to cut back the raised fibres. Do not use water-based wiping stains on veneers.

It is generally preferable to apply these stains with a brush, rather than a rag, because you can keep the wood wetter and brush out unevennesses and overlaps. Let the stain dry until the surface is just damp, then wipe it over with a clean soft cloth to remove excess pigment and spread it evenly. Overlaps are more easy to deal with than they are with penetrating stains because you can wet the surface again, with either solvent or a thin wash of the stain, and move the pigment around. Using the solvent medium alone will obviously remove some of the colour and lighten it.

Pigments look 'cheaper'. Because they obscure, even obliterate, the grain, they are good for disguising softwoods and making different woods resemble each other. Accentuating grain and getting shading effects is easier with these stains, because you have more surface control of the colour itself, but the colours are on the whole muddier and duller than those of the clear penetrating dyes, and not so light-fast.

Stain can be applied with a brush or rag; pigmented varieties (above) spread better with a brush, the penetrating kinds (below) with a rag.

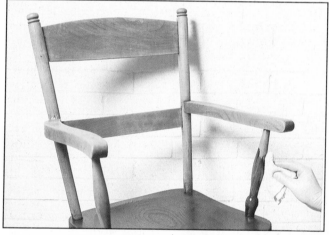

There is a wide range of natural colours in proprietary stains, and fabric or shoe dyes give a huge choice of brighter shades.

Penetrating stains

For raw wood, especially hardwoods, the penetrating stains or dyes are a better bet than pigmented stains. They are most commonly found on the market in an oil (naphtha) medium, whose solvent is white spirit. They are absorbed more evenly because they penetrate deeper into the wood, but, because of their penetration, it is more difficult to cure the common overlapping and splashing problems.

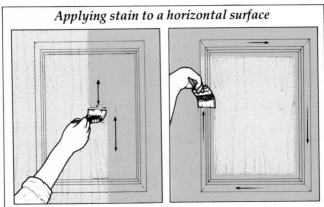

Applying stain to a horizontal surface

The correct and incorrect ways of applying stain. Always keep as few edges live as possible, especially on panels.

They also come in a range of proprietary wood colours, which can be mixed easily. These colours are very strong, and a mere hint of, say, black will darken a light shade considerably. Do not be tempted to mix two manufacturers' products together, even if they are both oil-based, because the other ingredients might not be compatible. Similarly, the colours themselves, though they might have the same name, differ in shade from brand to brand.

These stains are light-fast and give good, clear tones which do not obscure or obliterate the grain, but oil-based products absorbed into the wood do present the problem of 'bleeding' or 'striking through' the top finish, which, especially if it is varnish or polyurethane, will dissolve the medium and loosen the colour. Avoid this by applying a thin sealing coat of top finish and rubbing it back before you start the finish proper, and minimize it by rubbing the stained surface when it is dry with a clean cloth to remove the surplus dye.

On vertical surfaces, stain upwards to avoid runs.

It is best to use a rag to apply these stains, because it has a more even initial spread than a brush. Try to work across a surface so that only one edge is at its dampest ('live'); this gives you the best chance of blending. If you get a splash or drip, wipe it out as thin as possible *immediately*. If you do get unevenness, a careful application of the solvent will allow a bit of 'blendability', but only when it is not really dry and deeply absorbed. Once it is, the only solution is to sand the surface heavily to remove the top colour, then apply another coat. Semi-seal a surface that you know will probably absorb unevenly with a thin wash of top coat *before* you apply the stain: equal parts of raw linseed oil and white spirit make a good inhibiter for pine.

Penetrating stains and dyes are also available in aniline powder form, soluble in water, oil or methylated spirits. These give you greater flexibility and range of colour, but you will have to go to the trade houses to get them. They are old-style professional products, more relevant to restoration than production, and do demand an experienced touch. The spirit (meths) aniline stains dry in minutes and have to be applied with great skill.

Remember that you do not have to stick to wood-oriented products. Cold water fabric dyes dissolve well, and give you access to a whole range of startling colours, if you feel so inclined; shoe polish, applied like wax (see pp. 42-3), is also very effective.

Chemicals; mixing, colouring and tinting

The chemical reactions of acids and alkalis with the wood's own constituents give a deep-laid colour which is comparatively inexpensive and (in most cases) lasts well. These are traditional stains, the only ones available before modern industrial chemistry, and are still used in antique restoration or where, say, new church furniture has to be matched to very old. White vinegar

(acetic acid), if left with a handful of iron nails in it overnight, will turn oak almost black a matter of seconds after you apply it. A stain made from potassium permanganate crystals dissolved in water will bring out a warm brown shade, and makes a good dye for floors because it is inexpensive, although it does fade. Potassium bichromate crystals, which are yellow and orange, dissolved in warm water, darken oak, ash, mahogany and other high tannic acid-content woods without affecting the basic colour. Burnt sienna – a pigment – dissolves in stale beer and makes a very effective mahogany-coloured stain; and there are many more.

If you want to mix your own stain, start with a decision about the colouring agent and the base, and then experiment. Pigments are really best for touching up over an already sealed surface; water as a medium will give you problems with raised grain; slow-drying oils are easiest to apply evenly, but might strike through a finish; spirit-based dyes dry very quickly. Keep a careful record of the proportions you are using, and *always test*.

Touching in, painting grain lines over stopping (wood filler) and so on, is best done with oil (white spirit) and pigments – artist's oil pigments are fine. For french polishing, you can tint the finish by adding pigment or spirit aniline dyes to the shellac itself. Use a fine artist's brush, so that you can control exactly what colour goes where. Cellulose and synthetic lacquers have their own tinters. These fine touches should always be sealed on top; the order is stain, sealer, touch-in, finishing coats.

Coloured varnishes are already pigmented, and can be used to carry more. Used on their own, they are popular because they are not difficult to mix or apply but they are a quick compromise solution, and show up as such. There is nothing to recommend them in terms of appearance, in that they combine uneven pigment spread with the thick 'plastic on top' look of polyurethane. These too should be given a top coat of clear varnish or polyurethane, whichever you are using.

Left: *Traditional stains:* (from top) *white vinegar and iron nails; vandyke brown, ammonia and water; potassium permanganate crystals and warm water, all on oak; mahogany crystals and water; potassium permanganate crystals and warm water; burnt sienna and stale beer; potassium bichromate crystals and warm water, all on beech.*

Grain filling and bleaching

Bleaching is done before staining, grain filling after. You might have deep marks to remove, such as those that water makes on oak (a particularly reactive timber), or you might want to lighten the whole surface generally, especially if you have used a caustic soda stripper.

Bleach works well on open-grained hardwoods like ash, beech or elm, but not on the close-grained ones like cherry, rosewood or padauk. Neutralizing bleaches, like strippers, is vital; they are corrosive and dangerous, so be careful – always add crystals or solutions to water, not the other way round. Sand with medium grit paper (100) to open the grain before you bleach – you'll be sanding with finer papers afterwards – and do not bleach veneers.

The weakest and easiest to use is household bleach. Start with a weak solution to see how it works, then strengthen it if you need to. Mop it on, leave it to dry, and rinse it thoroughly with clean water and vinegar. Oxalic acid is the next in strength, and is widely used in the trade. It is good for removing water-stains from oak. Use 50g (2oz.) of crystals per 500 ml (1 pint) of hot water, mop it on hot, leave it to dry, and neutralize it with a solution of 1 part ammonia to 10 parts water. Two-part 'A & B' solution (a mix of hydrogen peroxide and ammonia or caustic soda) is very strong and quite dangerous. Apply the first coat, leave it for about 10 or 20 minutes, then apply the second. Neutralize – stop the action if you want to – with full strength vinegar. Do not use this solution on oak.

Grain filling aids your smooth build up of finish – the glassy feel – and, if you put it on right, it will not obscure the grain pattern. It also surface-levels the pores, which would otherwise give your clear finish a pitted effect, however many coats you put on.

Proprietary fillers come in a wide range of colours, and should be used one shade darker than the wood, which itself will darken as if it was wet when the clear finish is applied. Thin them to a paste for the hardwoods and a thick liquid for soft, open-grained pine, using the correct solvent – white spirit or meths. Rub in the filler with a coarse cloth across the grain, let it 'go off' – begin to dry – and then rub off the surplus, also across the grain, packing it hard into the pores. Finish by wiping hard along the grain.

Colour-matching any additions in this old pine kitchen must start with bleach. Only when you have got a neutral ground will you be able to build up the characteristic washed-out grey tones.

The thinner fillers should be pushed in with a brush. Leave them to dry for a day, then fine paper the surface down, and rub in raw linseed oil to clear the muddy appearance. Wipe the surplus off thoroughly.

You can mix your own filler with superfine plaster, french chalk, or silex (china clay). Use pigments or oil stains to colour it, and a solvent compatible with the colour and the top finish. This is especially important for cellulose, which has its own nitro fillers, and will not take to oils. There are shellac-based liquid fillers available for french polishing close-grained woods.

Wax and oil finishes

For ease of application and softness of sheen, wax and oil are hard to beat, but offer comparatively little surface protection. Both need constant maintenance, although both are easy to maintain. Many coats of wax, however, built up over the years, will yellow and obscure grain and colour, and will also collect grime. That definite but intangible glowing warmth of an old finish – patina – is the product of waxing, buffing and normal wear over the life of the piece, so if you do strip and rewax a surface, expect to take time to regain the patina.

These finishes are more attractive on hardwoods. Silicon waxes should be treated with caution, since they are incompatible with any other sort, and give much more of a 'household sparkle' than a warm finish. There are many good-quality traditional furniture wax blends on the market, which use carnauba, beeswax and other additives; use these. A word of warning – once wax is applied to a raw surface, you must give up the idea of using any other finish at all over it. You can strip it with white spirit (paint thinner), but some wax will certainly remain in the pores of the wood.

Use wax on pieces that get no hard wear, like carvings, decoration, marquetry, hall furniture and so on. It is also commonly applied inside drawers and cabinets, where its fragrance mixes with the wood's natural aroma, and on drawer sides to facilitate running.

Oil finishes give durable, deep-wood protection against heat and moisture, have a distinctive flat, dull sheen, and are the only treatments through which you can feel the grain texture. Application is easy, but demands a lot of time and work. Linseed is traditionally used, either raw, which takes a long time to dry, or boiled, which sets more quickly but becomes gummy during application. It soaks deep into the grain and hardens by oxidation, allowing the wood to shrink or expand freely. Oil forms no barrier to surface knocks or bruises, but is untouched by heat and liquids and can be easily touched up, which is why it is a good choice for table-tops. Teak, tung and Danish oils (penetrating wood sealers) carry added resins which leave a harder surface film; they do, however, require much more careful application than linseed.

Left: *A penetrating oil finish would be very suitable for this dresser* (top), *whose rustic style would be spoiled by a high gloss; wax over french polish would give a beautiful patina to the writing table* (bottom).

Wax application

Grain filler is not necessary if you are applying wax; the wax itself does the job most efficiently. To avoid many applications and an unnecessary amount of absorption, you can seal the surface first with a thin coat or two of shellac; rub it down with wire wool or fine garnet between coats. You can also increase protection deep in the fibres against heat and water by applying a warmed, thinned mix first. Melt 50/50 wax and white spirit in a can in a pan of hot water, stirring it to a thick liquid, and brush it in hard with a shoebrush. You might have to reheat it to keep it runny. Wipe off the residue, and when it has set, cut it back with wire wool, then apply full-strength, normal temperature coats with a soft rag. They will buff up easily.

It is usual to apply wax with a rag; wipe it on, leave it for a few minutes to 'go off', and buff. The main point is not to get lumps in the rag or on the surface, which will smear, and which can be avoided by making sure the wax is soft enough and warm enough to spread easily. Put on as many coats as it takes to bring up a deep shine, and expect to rewax a surface regularly. Once or twice a year, depending on how often you wax, you should clean as much off as you can with white spirit and start the build-up process again.

For pieces that get harder use, wax can be used as a 'disposable protection' skin over a clear finish. It gives a softness to an otherwise hard brilliance, and when applied with wire wool has the added advantage of removing the final nibs and giving a sheen at the same time. It is also a quick way of finishing low-wear surfaces which have been sealed with the economic minimum of lacquer or varnish.

Oil application

The traditional oil-finishing work schedule is daunting, to say the least: 'Once a day for a week, once a week for a month, once a month for a year, once a year for the rest of your life.' The principle, if not perhaps demanding quite such a taxing regime, is that you soak the wood until it will absorb no more, wipe off the surplus, leave it to set for 24 hours, paper it down, and soak it again. When it will take no more, or after a week, whichever comes first, buff it long and hard with a cloth wrapped in a brick. 'Top it up' regularly.

Liquid waxes with pigments have deep penetration, but melting beeswax and carnauba gives control over consistency, and a lighter tone.

There are ways round this off-putting schedule, such as using the 'oil-resin' finish. This is an equal-parts mixture of varnish, white spirit and linseed or proprietary oil, soaked, wiped, papered and burnished in the same way, which offers a particularly effective combination of flexibility and durability. The 'buffing with a brick' part – the extra weight gives extra friction – could be eased by fitting a cloth pad to an orbital sander; as with any finish, the result is in direct proportion to the amount of work you put in.

If you use the proprietary teak, tung or Danish oils, a first-class brush is every bit as important as for varnish application, if not more so. Brush the first coat on, using the techniques described on pp. 58-9, leaving a film which you should cut right back to the wood the next day. Then do three or four more coats, wire wooling each one, but merely de-nibbing, not rubbing back so much. Burnish with wax and wire wool, pumice or rottenstone. Extra penetration is achieved by laying these oils over an initial soaking of 50/50 raw linseed oil and white spirit.

Both these and linseed oils can be tinted with pigments, oil stains, or oil-soluble aniline dyes. *Beware seepage* – an oil-finished piece should stand on plastic until you are sure no more will seep from the legs on to the carpet!

French polishing

Introduction

Generally considered to be the most prestigious and desirable of all the clear finishes, french polish is the best
looking, but in many ways the least practical. Its depth
and brilliance are unequalled by varnishes or lacquers,
because the surface it forms is actually wafer-thin, and
gives grain pattern and colour a particular clarity,
almost a transparency.

The French Martin brothers developed a polish based
on shellac in the eighteenth century, a version of which
was being used in England for pianos by 1815. By the
late nineteenth century it had become the most popular
treatment for high-quality furniture and joinery, especially mahogany. This timber still looks beautiful french
polished, but other woods (though not wide-pored oak)
can be treated equally successfully.

French polish is resistant to neither heat nor liquids,
and is particularly susceptible to alcohol, so table tops
are usually waxed to ease maintenance. This is not to
say that the finish cannot be repaired at all (see pp. 24-
7) but rewaxing is a great deal easier and quicker.

There is a certain mystique about polishing, probably
because application with a rubber is an involved
process, and recognizing the stage it has reached
demands experience. Once you have developed a 'feel'
for the rubber, however, you will find that it is a great
deal easier than generations of craftsmen would have us
believe. Doing it is really the only way to learn.

If you are finishing a new piece there is very little to
be said for french polishing it, if it will be getting ordinary household use. But you will find it on antique, old
or reproduction furniture and will need to know how to
apply it when you are refinishing.

French polish is particularly reactive to damp; white
blotches will appear in the finish if you apply it in a
humid atmosphere, and it will not harden if the
temperature in your workspace is less than 15°C (60°F).
If conditions are bad and you still have to french polish,
fix up a non-flammable heater over the surface, or warm
it over with an iron on top of a blanket. This can also
eliminate damp patches in the wood fibres.

Left: *This curl mahogany veneer is greatly enriched by staining
before french polishing; without the colour, the surface would be
dull and lifeless. A wax layer over the final coat gives easily
maintained protection.*

Shellac

The basic ingredients of french polish are shellac and methylated spirits (wood alcohol). The secretions from the lac insect, found in India, Africa and the Far East, were originally used for red dye; while commercial chemistry has evolved better and cheaper colouring agents, there is still no synthetic equivalent of lac for french polish. The fluids secreted from the larvae encrust the twigs of infested trees; the 'stick lac' formed like this is harvested, pounded, melted, refined and filtered through 'seed' and 'lump' stages to make wafer-thin sheets. These sheets are then flaked and exported as shellac.

The decorative detail of these boxes would be best suited by the hardness and clarity of transparent white polish.

Types and mixes of french polish

The shellac/meths mix includes gums like arabic and copal, plus drying and hardening agents, to make the polish as it is sold. The off-the-shelf product is likely to be a '3lb cut' – in other words, 1.3kg (3lb) of shellac dissolved in 5l (1 gal.) of methylated spirits. The thicker '5lb cut', the other basic British mix, is for brushing, and is often sold as 'brush polish'. It is worth remembering these proportions when you are thinning or mixing different polishes for colouring or sealing.

French polishes come in a handful of basic varieties, according to the purity of the shellac; all can be intermixed, and both pigments and the clearer spirit aniline dyes can be used to tint them. Be careful, however, if a polish you buy is obviously a manufacturer's 'special'; it might have synthetic ingredients which demand special mixers. Always ask.

Button polish, so called because the shellac comes in little cakes or buttons, is brownish with a yellow tinge. Brown or 'orange' polish is a standard, made from orange shellac, and commonly known as just 'polish'. It is usually used for mahogany, as is garnet polish – a red- rather than a yellow-brown which gives clarity and warmth to mahogany that brown and button polish lack. White polish is milky in appearance and is made from acid-bleached shellac, which has a very limited shelf-life – two years at the absolute outside. It darkens the light woods on which it is used only slightly; there is no way of telling if it has deteriorated until you find it has not hardened after application, so buy only as much as you can predict you'll use. Transparent white is bleached twice, is clearer still than white polish, and is especially suitable for marquetry and inlays where no colour darkening at all is desirable.

You can buy ready-coloured polishes like red and black, and other proprietary makes may include acid or melamine hardeners for tables or bar-tops, or even exterior use. They are usually thicker, and formulated for application with a brush.

A '2lb cut' of white or transparent white polish is generally used as a sealing coat to protect stain from bleeding, or just to limit the absorbency of the wood before final finishing. Varnish can be put over shellac, but never for outside use; cellulose and the synthetic lacquers, which have their own 'sanding sealers', will not 'take' over shellac.

Making and using a rubber

Although you can use mops, brushes and spray guns for french polish, by far the most important method of application is with the rubber. This is no more than an absorbent pad, but making a good one and mastering its behaviour are essential to good french polishing.

Take a piece of cotton wadding, about 25cm (10in.) × 12.5cm (5in.), and fold it in half to make a square. Fold across three of the corners to make a pointed oblong, then place it on a fine, clean white rag. A well-washed linen handkerchief is ideal; it must be lint-free, colourless, and have no embroidery or stitching that might mar the surface.

Fold the rag over the pointed front of the wadding, then fold the sides in. The rest of the rag should be folded over the back of the wadding and screwed up so the lump rests in the palm of your hand. You should be able to squeeze the wadding by screwing the linen on top up more tightly, and it should also be easy to unfold the linen so you can charge the rubber.

Polish is dripped into the wadding from the top with the linen folded back. There must be no creases or folds, which will leave uneven marks and troughs in the surface, in the base of the rubber. Hold the rubber gently but firmly, with your fingers all round it to keep the shape and the flat base. When polishing a horizontal surface, drop your wrist so the weight of your arm works parallel rather than at an angle to the surface; this is especially important for circular motions, where there is a tendency to press harder on the outer sweep than the inner. Even pressure is vital.

Charging the rubber correctly is also important. Drip some polish into it a little at a time then dab the rubber on some (clean!) scrap wood to bring the polish through. It must not be so wet that too much polish flows, but if it is too dry the friction will cause the rubber to stick. An even flow is just as vital as even pressure, so as the charge is used up, press harder on the rubber to keep the same amount coming out. It is a common mistake at first to overcharge the rubber and not press hard enough: just wiping over the surface is no good, because the damp polish holds the rubber back and makes the action jerky. In the initial stages, you are forcing the polish into the grain, while in the latter, friction itself plays an important part in getting the brilliance of the finish.

The rubber

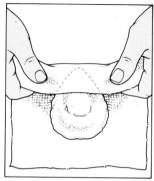

1 Fold the rag over the pointed front of the wadding.

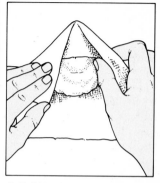

2 Fold in the sides so they leave a pear-shaped point.

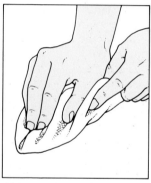

3 Screw up the remaining rag into your palm.

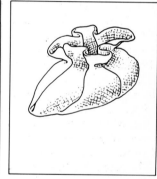

4 The pear-shaped point is for getting into corners.

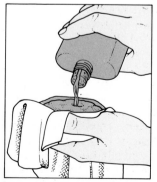

5 A v-groove cut in the cork helps to control the flow.

6 Keep the weight of your arm parallel to the surface.

Applying french polish

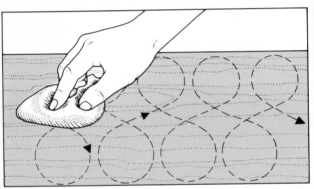

1 Bodying up: first apply the polish in overlapping circles, and glide on and off the surface at the sides and edges.

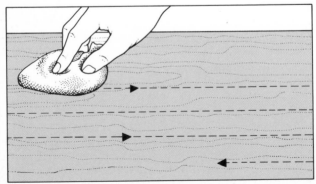

2 Next, apply polish in a figure-of-eight movement; even pressure and flow are vital.

3 Spiriting off removes the cloudiness of the oil; sweep the meths rubber along the grain.

Bodying up and spiriting off

The first operation, 'skinning in' or 'fadding', coats the grain with shellac. Charge the rubber and wipe it across the grain in straight, overlapping strokes, then do the same along the grain. Aim for even pressure and flow. A whistling sound from the rubber indicates there is a crease or fold, which you must deal with immediately.

The next stage is bodying up. First apply the polish in overlapping circles, going along, down, along and down again. Then lay more polish on in a figure-of-eight movement; if you see ridges building up as a result of uneven pressure, go back to moving straight along the grain to wipe them down. If you cannot wipe the ridges away, leave them to harden and paper them back. Try not to recharge the rubber in the middle of one going-over of the surface; as the polish is used up, press harder until you have finished one covering, then recharge.

Five or six applications, waiting only a minute or two between each, should be enough to build up an even coat, filling the grain and leaving a body of polish. In this part of the process you will find the rubber wanting to drag. Lubricate it by rubbing a fingertip's worth of raw linseed oil on the pad, using as little as possible because its cloudiness must be removed later.

After these bodying coats, leave the work to harden, preferably overnight. The polish will have sunk somewhat and you will be able to feel any imperfections. Wipe the surface carefully with fine, worn garnet paper, clean it meticulously, and do some more bodying until there is no hint of grain texture to the touch. You might need another five or six applications; in the last two, charge the rubber with 75/25 polish/meths, then 50/50. Depending on how much oil you have used, the surface will be smooth but smeary, and by now well-built-up.

Spiriting off removes the cloudiness of the oil. Make a new rubber, with three or four layers of rag this time, and charge it with meths so it is just damp enough to feel cold on your cheek. Sweep the meths rubber along the grain; it will lift the oil, which will form a tide-mark round the edges of the linen, out. If the surface clears then clouds over again, you are merely moving the oil around, not lifting it out, and you will have to take the dirty rag off and use the clean one underneath.

Go through these stages until you have a clear, brilliant, french polished surface.

Hints and problems

A finished french polished surface should be left at least a week to harden before you use it. Wax will protect it, but reduce the brilliance a little; if you want an eggshell or a flatter finish, apply pumice with a felt pad and oil or rottenstone powder dry with a dulling brush (furniture rubbing brush). Be extremely gentle; if you use oil, wipe it off and buff the surface with a clean soft cloth.

For awkward corners, mouldings and carvings, you can apply polish with a soft bear-, squirrel- or sable-hair mop, or use glaze, which is easy to apply and quick-drying. In fact a spirit varnish (gum benzoin in meths), glaze can be bought from trade suppliers. It is, however, less durable than polish itself. Lay a body of polish, then finish off with two or three coats of glaze, allowing them to harden properly between applications.

For the insides of cabinets and desks, where you want to seal and protect the surface but do not need a full french polished finish, use dry shining. This is basic polishing, without the grain filling or the use of oil. Fad and body enough just to fill the grain, using straight then circular strokes; after three or four applications, charge the rubber slightly more fully than usual and finish off with long, even strokes. Oil would have to be spirited off, defeating the whole object of speed and ease, so do not use any, but be extra careful to prevent the rubber sticking.

'Stiffing' is a technique for cabinet interiors and other areas where you cannot glide on and off the edges. Start at the edges and work towards the middle, lifting the rubber as you get there to overlap a stroke you have made from the other side. It takes a lot of practice to be able to do this without building up ridges; if you do get some, they can be smoothed very delicately with a spirit rubber after about half an hour's hardening time.

Lubricating a french polish rubber with oil can be less controlled than just lubricating one sticky area of the surface, which many professionals prefer to do. Always be sparing with oil, and do not use it unless you really have to. Do not keep worrying away at a problem area, it will only get worse. Leave it to harden a few minutes and then see whether a wipe with polish will smooth it out. If not, paper it back when it's hard.

Make sure there is no dampness in the surface. When repolishing an old piece, dismantle it as far as possible,

Though the polish of this low-boy is pitted and marked, the superb patina makes it unwise to strip and repolish the piece.

taking off removable mouldings and marking them so they go back in the same place. Mount them on a strip of hardboard and fix them to a board to work on them, so the edges are held away from the surface. If you have stained a repair to match in and it lightens under the polish, tint some polish and brush that over the area, let it harden and seal it with a thin coat, then continue over the whole surface. If you are making panelled doors, try to polish the panel before you glue up the frame – the glue will not adhere to the polish, and there will be no problem getting your rubber into the corners. Otherwise you must use the pear-shaped point of the rubber.

Make up felt- or blanket-covered battens to protect a polished surface when you have to do the other side; pad vice (vise) jaws like this too. Do not trail your shirt-buttons, jewellery or a loose edge of rag from the rubber over the work; keep your hands as free from flaky dried shellac as possible; pour polish and oil well away from the work; and, above all, start on small, unimportant surfaces and move on to more ambitious projects as you get the feel of the rubber and the polish.

Varnishes

Introduction

Varnish is basically paint without pigment. It is a high-resin-content finish, traditionally based on oil (turpentine) or spirit and using natural gums like copal and benzoin; there is no real advantage in these old-fashioned materials, which are slower drying and less durable than the wide range of synthetic resin varnishes on the market.

The most common types available today are polyurethane and marine varnish. Alkyds and vinyls are also used in resin manufacture, although more for the American than the British market. Polyurethanes come in one- or two-pack solutions (the latter are often called lacquers) and are extremely hard and durable, which makes them excellent for household use. Precisely because of their hardness, however, they do have weaknesses; they do not allow the wood to move, and will crack and peel if moisture is absorbed through a chipped edge or any break in the film. They build up very thickly, and give the wood a plastic-like appearance which tends to detract from its beauty. They are also surprisingly difficult to apply well.

Marine or 'spar' varnishes use phenolic resins, and remain comparatively soft and flexible, allowing the wood to expand and contract without cracking. They are designed for exterior use and they tend to yellow with age more than the polyurethanes. Alkyds are less expensive, less durable, but easier to apply and build up smoothly; vinyls are the clearest and dry more quickly than the others, but are not so tough.

Varnishes are applied in much the same way as household paint, and for this reason they have the widest 'non-trade' market. Very little emphasis is given by the manufacturers to the difficulties and demands of good varnish application, which is why badly varnished furniture and fittings are often seen in the household; too little attention has been paid to cleaning the work, and using the right brush in the right way.

All the common synthetic varnishes are available in high gloss, satin or matt finishes, but the proportions of resins, and thus the eventual appearance of the finished product, does vary from manufacturer to manufacturer.

Left: *Polyurethane varnish is often used in the home, particularly in high-wear areas like stairs, hallways and front doors. Careful preparation and delicate brushwork are essential.*

Choice, use and care of varnish brushes

The quality of your varnish finish depends on your brushes, and your choice and care of them must reflect your desire for the very best results. It is all too easy to neglect the brush and remain perplexed why you cannot get a perfect finish.

Buy a very good brush, and keep it for varnish only. A good width is 50-65mm (2-2½in.), although you will need something narrower for thin mouldings or frame members; natural bristle is on the whole better than synthetic. It should have a tapered shape and a good thickness of bristles, a proportion of them with flagged tips. The wedge between the two rows should not be

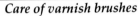

Care of varnish brushes

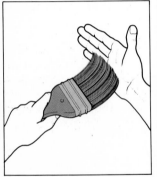

1 *Slap the bristles back and forth against your hand.*

2 *Straighten them with a wide-toothed comb.*

3 *Suspend brushes overnight in a varnish/solvent mix.*

4 *Tamp the bristles hard to the heel in solvent.*

too wide, or it will keep them separate and prevent the brush from holding a good charge that will flow nicely.

A new brush will always shed bristles when it is first used. Dip it in a mixture of varnish and white spirit (paint thinner) and work the bristles hard against a piece of scrap wood, slap it against the edge of your hand, then dip it and scrub it on the wood again. Straighten out the bristles before they have a chance to set in a tangle. It is also worth drilling a hole in the handle and suspending the bristles from a piece of wire across the top of the jar in a 50/50 varnish/solvent mix.

This 'keeper' will also be ideal for work that goes on over several days, allowing you to have the brush ready and not spend time cleaning it after each session. Never stand a brush on its bristles in the jar, they will take on a permanent bend. You can keep a brush soft overnight by soaking it in solvent and wrapping the bristles tightly in silver foil, but these are temporary measures, and not a substitute for proper cleaning.

When you do finally clean the brush, do not skimp. Wipe it hard on newspaper or rags, then pour about 12mm (½in.) of solvent into a shallow tin or jar and tamp the brush in it, replacing the cleaner often. Go on doing it until there is no more varnish coming out of the bristles – it stays up by the handle, so be patient. Comb the bristles straight if they are tangled.

Problems with varnish

Apart from the quality of your brush, the other major obstacle to getting a good varnish finish is dust. It is more your enemy with varnish than anything else, because of the slow drying times involved. Damp the floor and sweep up thoroughly first, then try to avoid moving dust at all – even near the room in which you are working – during the whole process. After sanding, clean the work minutely with white spirit and a tack rag. It is inevitable that specks will stick to the coats, but they can be cut back with fine garnet or wet and dry paper, apart from those in the very last coat. If you have the highest standards, de-nib the final coat with wax and wire wool, or for a high gloss, rub it well with rottenstone, felt pad and oil. You can de-nib a satin finish without glossing it by gently stroking the finest wire wool over it, or using the fine abrasive pastes like T-cut or toothpaste. Do not rub the surface so much that it burnishes to a gloss.

Applying varnish

Delicate brushwork is essential for good results with varnish. There is no question of slapping it on and brushing it out like paint; the first thinned coats sink into the grain and then you lay coat on top of successive smooth coat.

Never dip the brush into the can more than one-third or half of the bristles' length. Do not shake the can – this will cause air bubbles that hold in the liquid and pop on the surface – stir it firmly but smoothly. For the same reason, do not scrape the bristles on the rim of the can to unload excess, tap them lightly against the edge.

As far as possible, have the surface you are working on horizontal. Set the work up on supports so that you will not have to move it during varnishing. With awkward pieces like chairs, do the difficult parts first so you do not have to reach over a wet part to get at an untouched area. With framed panels, start with the moulding, keeping the brush strokes in the direction of the grain, then do the panel, then blend the moulding into the frame members round it. On flat surfaces, work from a wet area towards a dry, and blend the overlaps when the brush is not so fully charged.

Try to get long, smooth sweeps of the brush from one end of the surface to the other. If this is impossible, use the 'stiffing' technique (see p. 52). Once you have put on a 50/50 thinned coat and cut it back, the varnish will not sink appreciably into the grain, but will form a skin and lose 'brushability' quite quickly. You should be flowing it on, not brushing it in. Thin the second coat 20 per cent, then go to full strength for the top coats.

When you lay a coat down, remember that the skin must not be given a chance to form before you have smoothed the whole coat, so work quickly and deftly. You can only get rid of brushmarks while the coat is at its wettest, with the brush held nearly vertical and by stroking the tips over the area. If the varnish is even faintly tacky, the marks will stay, and you will have to cut them right back with garnet or wet and dry when the coat is hard. Be very watchful for drips and runs on corners and edges, brushing away from them once they are covered.

Rub each coat down with worn fine garnet or wet and dry paper and clean it meticulously with a tack rag before the next. Some polyurethanes are supposed to be recoated within a certain time so that the coats fuse, and

Laying a coat of varnish

1 Tap the bristles against the rim to unload excess.

2 To lay a coat down, start by brushing along the grain.

3 Respread it with the tips of the bristles across the grain.

4 Finish with a feather-light touch along the grain again.

there is no need for sanding, but this is very difficult to judge, and you can easily pull up the previous coat. It is safer to allow the previous application to harden, rub it down and reapply, but be sure to do it thoroughly – polyurethane's hardness does cause adhesion problems.

Two-pack polyurethanes are even harder than the single-packs, and are usually used on floors. Sand thoroughly between coats for the sake of adhesion. Some of these finishes are advertised as having the wear- and liquid-resistance of plastic, and indeed they do, but they also look like it, which makes them a doubtful choice for furniture. They are also extremely unpleasant to use, and their strong toxic fumes make a face-mask and eye protection essential.

Lacquers

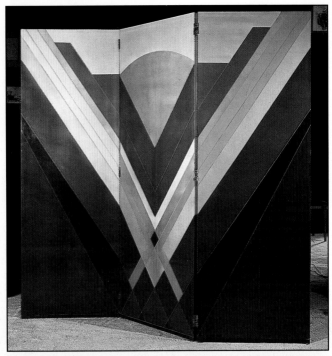

The lacquer finishes

Nitro-cellulose and synthetic lacquers are by far the commonest finishes in industry, because of their fast application and drying. There are brushing varieties, which are thicker and slower-drying for even 'flowing on', but generally spraying is best. You can cover large areas in a very short time and, with careful and thorough rubbing down between coats, achieve a superbly smooth finish quite easily.

These materials take between 30 and 60 minutes to dry reasonably hard, and many can be recoated after that time; full curing takes at least a day, and in some cases a week, after which they are among the hardest and most durable of all finishes.

Cellulose is made from nitro-cellulose, resins, plasticizers and thinners; pre-catalysed lacquers include cellulose, melamine, and acid hardeners, but the synthetic resin-carrying and acid-catalysed lacquers, the toughest of all, need to be mixed with a hardening catalyst immediately before application.

Cellulose finishes offer no advantages over pre- or acid-catalysed lacquers, apart from a certain extra flexibility allowing movement of the wood. They all come in satin, matt or gloss finishes, and should be used with water-based stains and fillers, or ones that use the same solvents as the lacquers themselves. Like spirit-based products, nitro-stains and fillers are easy to use and mix. If you do use oil- or spirit-based stains and fillers, seal them well with at least two coats of the lacquer you use; and wait and watch for a possible reaction or bleeding through. Avoid laying these lacquers over shellac or varnish.

Lacquers can be tinted with their own colours, or you can use cellulose-based enamels for car touch-up work underneath them.

The hardness of these products, particularly acid-catalysed lacquers, makes them ideal for ordinary household use. They are resistant to mild acids and alkalis and stand up to knocks and heat very well – although damp heat like steam corrupts pre-catalysed lacquers fairly easily.

Left: *Do not rule out lacquers just because they are not on the home-user market and require spraying. Trade suppliers will sell small amounts, and investment in a spray outfit is worth it if you are serious about the work.*

Spray guns and spraying

Dirt is the biggest bugbear of spraying. Nozzles, tubes and liquids should be spotless; soak the parts in thinners and strain your lacquers through a single thickness of nylon stocking. Having carefully prepared your surface, damp all dust and sweep up thoroughly, then disturb it no more.

Practise spraying on a large piece of flat panel until you have a flat fan of spray, which will coat an area 35-45cm (15-18in.) wide with the gun held 20-30cm (8-12in.) from the surface at 90° to it. It is easier to spray a vertical surface than a horizontal one. Wait a minute to see the effect on your test surface, because lacquer takes some time to run if it is going to. Thin it 10 per cent and get the right consistency by timing it through a viscosity cup. The liquid should flow in a continuous stream off the end of a stick held at 45°.

Spraying techniques are illustrated opposite. Never trigger or stop the gun while it is pointing at the surface. Start the spray, and stop it, off the panel at the beginning and end of your strokes. Do internal corners in one smooth movement; external corners should have one stroke each side and one at a 45° angle.

Pre-catalysed lacquers can be de-nibbed with 600 grit wet and dry paper and water, wiped and tack-ragged after 45-60 minutes, and are then ready for recoating. Acid-catalysed lacquers take longer, about three hours on average. Final coats should be steel wool and waxed, or rubbed with burnishing cream.

Damp in the air causes a milky bloom as the lacquer dries. Burnish it with abrasive cream or paste, or if that does not work strip and refinish. Spray will pick up moisture in a cold damp atmosphere and take it to the surface, where it mixes with the lacquer, causing pits and craters in the finish, with the same white bloom. The air must be dry and warm, but if it is too hot it will dry the lacquer too quickly.

Always clean the gun as if it was a surgical instrument. Dismantle it, soak all the parts in thinners and blow thinners through the gun until there is not a trace of lacquer in the spray.

Finally, take elaborate safety precautions. Fine spray vapours are highly volatile, and extremely unpleasant to inhale; always wear a face mask, have a good extraction system, or do the work outside. Just having the windows open is not nearly enough.

Spraying techniques

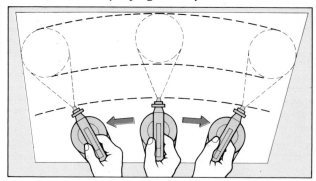

1 Do not vary the distance of the gun from the surface by moving in an arc.

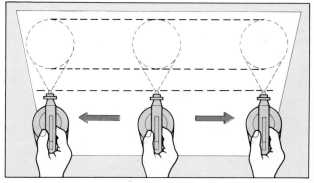

2 Keep the gun at a constant 20-30cm (8-12in.) from the surface, as if it were on rails.

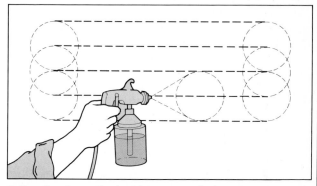

3 Overlap the strokes by 50 per cent – the liquid fan is much thinner at the extremities.

Specials

Antiquing, shading and glazes

Decorative finishes are currently enjoying a great revival, and in the world of fashion at least, no longer is it unacceptable to contrive obvious effects on furniture, panels and fittings. In this range of work, experimentation is absolutely essential; you will never be sure just how the materials are going to blend or conflict until you try. *Always* keep several large pieces of scrap so you can try your ideas out before you commit them to wood.

Glazing is a basic colour-wiping technique that you will use time and time again in antiquing, graining, shading and many other effects. A translucent tint, either contrasting or matching, is wiped over a (usually) matt base coat. The tint must be reasonably quick-drying, but allow time to be manipulated. Liquid glazes are available from art suppliers, but you can mix your own; use 1 part boiled linseed oil to 2 parts white spirit (paint thinner) plus pigments, or 1 part varnish to between 3 and 5 parts white spirit, plus pigments. Oil slows the drying process, but if there is too much, the protective top coat will pick up the glaze, smear and ruin it. Too little oil will cause the glaze to dry too quickly, and make wiping and shading difficult.

Raw umber and raw sienna are the pigments most commonly used in antiquing glazes. A standard antique white finish, for instance, uses: two coats of matt ivory or off-white paint on a smoothly sanded surface, rubbed down between coats and left to dry; a glaze pigmented with yellow ochre, burnt umber and a touch of white, brushed on then wiped off high spots like turnings, mouldings, and the centres of panels, then blended with a dry brush while it is still wet; and finally a protective coat of varnish, also perhaps tinted with burnt umber to dull it down.

You can use as a wiping coat, artist's oil paints, house paint, pigments in oil and white spirit, coloured varnish, tinted Danish oil, or shellac, all thinned for translucency. Your imagination and taste are the only limiting factors. If the finished effect is not convincing, wipe the whole thing off and start again; you will accumulate experience in wiping the right amount off the right areas.

Left: *Special effects with opaque finishes are as varied as they are fascinating. Simple glazing – green over ivory in this case – contrasts with the masterly lacquerwork of the cabinet.*

Textures, graining and distressing

One of the most notorious techniques of the antiquer or faker is 'distressing', which basically involves abusing new furniture to give it the dents, scratches and worn look of age. You can beat furniture with hammers and chains, drill tiny insect holes, burn it with cigarette ends, rub ash and cinders into it, scratch it, bake it, or – perhaps simplest of all – leave it outside for a week or two. Make sure all the joints are sound before you begin the finishing work. In all these and the other decorative techniques, *do not overdo it*.

Pine is particularly suited to texturing effects, because of the marked difference between its soft spring growth and the harder, darker summer wood. True 'pickling' uses a lethal caustic mixture which is allowed to eat into the wood, then hosed off – this is not for the beginner! Easier, less dangerous, pickle pine finishes include proprietary weathered pine stains; grey flat paint brushed on and wiped off, leaving a deposit in the pores, then sealed with shellac or varnish and waxed; wiped silvery grey or green glazes on brown or grey thin base coats; oxalic acid or two-part bleaches, neutralized, sanded, sealed with a thin coat of shellac, lightly stained and finished with tinted varnish or shellac. A solution of 1 part sulphuric acid to 3 parts water, applied to wet new pine, will give the orangey-brown colour of older pine. Neutralize with ammonia.

Straightforward brushing with a hard wire brush will remove soft wood and emphasize the harder grain pattern, more in pine than any other timber; sandblasting is even more effective, but obviously only for the professionally equipped. A modern version of the 'sugi' technique from Japan can be achieved by using a blowtorch before the wire brush – carefully wipe the flame over the surface then brush the charred timber out. Experiment first; have a bucket of water and a damp cloth ready and remember that heat builds up in wood, which could start to smoulder after you have moved on to another area. Strip off old finishes first!

Grain pattern can also be faked with glazes and a comb. The base coat of flat paint should be lighter, the glaze coat darker; do have a piece of the wood or a photograph for reference. Combs can be made from board or tin, the teeth cut to the size you want; you can buy rubber graining combs, or cut lumps out of old brushes. Graining technique is illustrated opposite.

Graining

1 Brush the glaze on, in lines for authenticity.

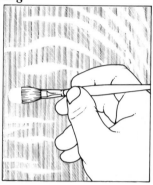

2 Brush across the lines to blur them.

3 Imitate the grain's pattern and curves with a comb.

4 When the glaze has dried, add darker lines with a feather.

While perfect simulation is unnecessary (and usually impossible), graining techniques should at least echo a specific timber's pattern and texture.

Marbling and scumbling

Marbling is one of the most enjoyable decorative techniques because all the material-compatibility rules are thrown out of the window. It is the use of varnishes, water- and oil-based paints, enamels, shellac, and various solvents in varying combinations, giving the distinctive separation of colours.

Marbling paper is astonishingly easy; just float waterproof inks or thinned enamels on the surface of a tray of water, and lay heavy paper into it. Lift it out, and you have a marbled surface which you can glue inside drawers; or on to furniture panels. Varnish over it for protection. The colours should float on the water without dispersing, but not on the other hand be so heavy that they sink. Trays and wooden panels can be treated like this, but give them a flat base coat of paint first; small pieces of furniture can also be submerged, half at a time if they are too big to go in all at once. The bath is an obvious tank, if you can face the cleaning up afterwards!

Marbling fire-surrounds, doors, larger pieces of furniture, and even walls, involves techniques far too numerous to list comprehensively, but the point is that your experimentation is as good as anyone else's. Do

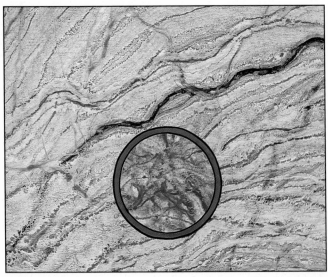

Make sure you have good reference for marbling: 'fidget' the dark lines in with the ragged edge of a feather.

not go wild and always have good reference – the real thing or photographs. A flat off-white or cream base coat is the starting point for the light grey and cream shades, followed by a glaze of artist's oils in white spirit. Use the colours you see in the natural stone. 'Scumble' or sponge and dab it; 'fidget' it with thin or broad dry brushes; and add the veins with black, grey or green paint applied with the edge of an old feather or a tiny brush.

The tank-floating technique can be reversed on to flat surfaces of furniture, as long as they are horizontal while you work. You can create the effect on ply or hardboard (masonite) panels, which you then set in or attach to the piece in question. Lay a 50/50 linseed oil/white spirit medium on to the surface, and float thinned enamels or oils on to it while it is still wet. They should be thicker in consistency than the base. Manipulate them with knives, brushes or pads; roll up a cloth with wodges of different colour in it, and roll it across the surface; drip pools of oil colour on to the surface and spread them out in wispy effects. Scumble it with a tissue, or crumpled newspaper rolled around on it. Keep the surface wet enough so the colours may be manipulated, but don't allow them to get muddy. When it is dry, seal it with two coats of varnish.

Lighter tones use an ivory base and a darker glaze. Let it 'go off' before scumbling with sponge or crumpled paper.

In this open-sided chest (above), the oak drawers are fumed while the frame has been left in stylish contrast. If you can use french polish, the rich deep black of real ebony (below) is not difficult to simulate; the wood must be close-grained and textured.

Ebonizing, fuming and liming

Beech is traditionally the wood used to imitate ebony, and it must be close- and even-grained. You need to get a very dense, rich black, so use dyes with good penetration; water-soluble anilines sink in more deeply if you add just a touch of ammonia. You must also use black filler – for oil stains, use black-pigmented dental plaster, mixed with some of the stain itself. Rub the filler hard into the grain, wiping it across and along, clear it with linseed oil, seal with transparent shellac if you have used an oil stain, and then french polish, using black polish, or aniline spirit black dissolved in white polish. If it is not black enough, add more spirit aniline dye, already dissolved, and a touch of laundry blue to give the blackness some life. Black cellulose or synthetic lacquers can also be sprayed on, as long as the stains and filler are carefully sealed; always put on a final transparent coat. Dulling an ebonized finish with pumice and a brush must be done very carefully, to get the straight lines parallel without overlapping.

Fuming is a remarkably simple method of darkening wood, almost always oak. The technique consists of putting the piece of furniture into a hermetically sealed space and surrounding it with saucers of .880 (point eight-eighty) ammonia. The fumes cause a deep reaction, but fading is quite quick and so the surface must be sealed as soon as you take it out of the ammoniac atmosphere. Small items can be fumed in a sealed cupboard and checked by plugging a peg of the same wood as you are fuming in a hole drilled in the side. If you want to do a large piece, fix up a polythene tent; sealing the seams and edges might be awkward, but checking is easy through the clear plastic. If some parts of the piece are darker than others, seal them with a thin coat of white polish and put it back in the fumes until the colour is even.

Liming is also used almost exclusively on oak and gives it a pale whitish-grey cast. Wire brush the grain to open the pores, and mix a creamy paste in the proportion of 1kg (2lb) of lump lime to 3.5 litres (6 pints) of water. Brush it in stiffly, forcing it into the pores; wipe the excess off, let it dry, paper it lightly and seal it with transparent polish or clear varnish. A 50/50 thinned white oil-based paint brushed on, worked in and wiped off does the job equally well. Sand and seal it in the same way.

The 'oriental look', gilding and stencilling

The pure-coloured, deep, thick 'lacquer' appearance of old japanned work can be easily created without delving into age-old oriental techniques. The more coats of varnish you put over a colour, the deeper the finish will be. It is vital to rub down meticulously between coats with 600 grit wet and dry paper and water, or, for the final coat especially, pumice, rotten-stone and oil. Enamels have the purest colours, and should be laid on at least two coats thick, then covered with up to six coats of varnish.

The patient preparation of the base surface is essential; you can try 'gesso' coatings for a perfectly flat base, either a proprietary acrylic product or inert powders like flour or decorator's filler added to paint. This covering is good for textured effects too. Tint the varnish with oil paints or oil-soluble aniline dyes, either to contrast or blend with the basic colour. Experiment with different colours in alternate varnish coats; on a red base, for instance, alternate blue and yellow-tinted varnishes will build up an unusually transparent green. These modern materials can equal the depth and beauty of the old lacquers, and are much more durable.

Adding stencilled patterns in these or other finishes is fairly simple, although if you choose to do it in more than one colour, the technique is more demanding. The paint you use to stencil must adhere well to the base, which is why matt is best, but you can key a gloss coat

The stained pattern on this floor is easily stencilled, but the inlaid lacquer of the chest is the fruit of a lifetime's work.

Gilding

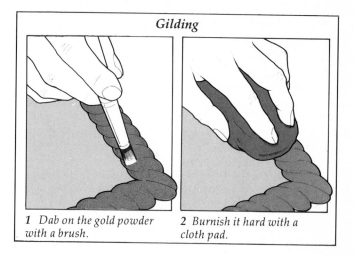

1 *Dab on the gold powder with a brush.*

2 *Burnish it hard with a cloth pad.*

by wire wooling through the stencil itself, and enamels, acrylics or water-based paints with good clear colour can all be used. Multiple-colour patterns need a stencil for each colour, all traced off a master drawing and carefully registered so they fit together on the surface.

Acetate is the best stencil material for the more ambitious designs so you can see exactly where you are painting. Use a stiff round brush, and lay thin coats of paint on top of each other rather than one thick one, since runs under the edges of the stencil will mean you have to lift it off and wipe them. Always varnish over a pattern to protect it. Borders can be very effective round a floor area; if you want a light pattern on a dark floor, seal the stencilled pattern with varnish or shellac and then stain the floor, wiping the colour off the non-absorbent decoration.

For gilding and the decorative metallic finishes often seen on carvings, edges and mouldings, gilt paste wax rubbed into selected areas, buffed, and burnished will give an antique look. Metallic paints wiped like this and rubbed well in are more effective than when they are merely painted. Put the metallic powders in glazes for wiping back, or carry them in suspension in built-up coats of varnish for a deep iridescence. For highly carved picture frames and mouldings where you want the gold or silver as solid as possible, coat the area with shellac then dust the powder on thickly with the brush while it is still wet, and burnish it hard with a cloth pad when it has dried.

Crackle, craze and other textures

Not unlike marbling, crackle or craze effects break the finishing rules on purpose; the very faults you try to avoid in spraying clear lacquers are the effects you seek.

The process involves using two coats which dry at different speeds. As the slower-drying base coat stretches and hardens, the quicker-drying top coat has already lost flexibility, and cracks and crazes in random, uncontrolled patterns. For clear finishes, you must use a spray gun, probably for the base coat but certainly for the top crackle enamel, which is a special preparation sold as such. Thin the crackle coat with the correct solvent to get the size and amount of broken areas you want. Spray on the top coat when the lower one is at exactly the right stage of drying; too wet, and it will sink in and make a wrinkled mess which you must strip, too dry and the stretching and crackling will not occur. It should have a 'skin', but not be tacky. The two coats must also obviously be solvent-compatible.

Use colours imaginatively in this kind of finish. Tint the base coat, or use a coloured enamel; try red on black or vice versa, green on gold, blue on red. A home-made version of this effect can be obtained using water-based emulsion paints (latex) over a quick-drying enamel or varnish. Brush the emulsion on only when a skin has formed on the base coat. If the base is too wet, the top paint will disperse in lacy loops; too dry and it will not adhere. For a wider choice, coat any coloured paints, when they are dry, with clear varnish, then lay the crackle coat into the varnish while it is drying. Wipe more colour into the crackle if you wish and seal everything with two coats of varnish.

Wrinkle effects also demand special materials which are treated with heat. Some are supposed to work without being put in an oven, but even a domestic heat source placed near them will help. A cellulose or synthetic lacquer on paint, enamel or varnish, will have just the same effect. Do make sure the solvents are safe together, as well as incompatible!

An oriental screen effect using reds and blues on a wiped gold surface is also very attractive, and easy to achieve. Dip a long nail in the coloured paint, and blow drips off it on to the gold surface with compressed air. Ring the changes in these colours too; blowing across a still-wet metallic paint with compressed air will mottle the surface and give it a hammered appearance.

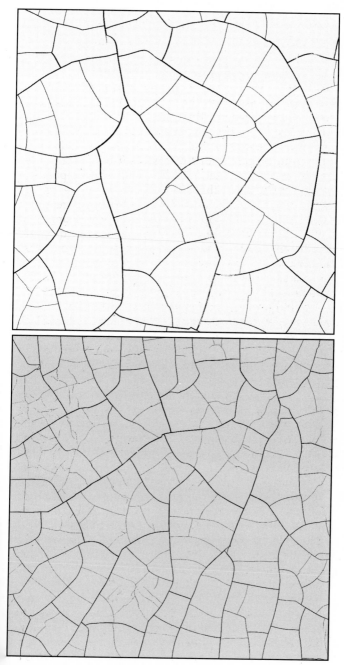

*Two drying rates, or basic incompatibility, create these textures.
You must apply the top coat at exactly the right moment.*

Acknowledgements

Swallow Books gratefully acknowledge the assistance given to them in the production of *Wood Polishing and Finishing Techniques* by the following people and organizations. We apologize to anyone we may have omitted to mention.

Photographs: Jon Bouchier 9, 12, 13, 28, 33(T), 36; The Bridgeman Art Library 40(T), 46, 53, 60(T), 70(B); Henry Flack (1860) Limited 4, 44; Noel Gaskell 70(T); Tim Imrie 64 (FP); International Paint 1, 6(L), 7(R), 30, 33(C); Roger Newton 68, 69; Nella Opperman 75; Ronseal 6(R), 7(L), 16, 25, 33(B), 40(B), 43, 54; Simon Stocker 60(B); Jessica Strang 39; Elizabeth Whiting and Associates 64(I) – photographer Spike Powell, designer Norma Bradbury, 67 – photographer Tom Leighton, 72 – photographer David Cripps, designer Lynn Le-Grice.
(T) – Top; (B) – Bottom; (FP) Full page; (L) – Left; (R) Right; (C) – Centre; (I) – Inset.

Tools on page 9 supplied by E. Amette and Co Ltd.
Photograph on page 36, materials used are manufactured and supplied by John Myland Limited, incorporating Gedge and Company, 80 Norwood High Street, London SE27 9NW.

Illustrations: Hussein Hussein 11, 23, 24, 26, 27, 56, 59, 63, 73; Aziz Khan 20, 34; Coral Mula 9, 19, 21, 22, 29, 35, 49, 50, 67; Rob Shone 15.

We are grateful to the London College of Furniture for their assistance in the preparation of this book.